Managing AI Risk

A practical approach to responsibly managing
AI with ISO 42001

Managing AI Risk

A practical approach to responsibly managing
AI with ISO 42001

ANDREW PATTISON

GRC Solutions
Unit 3, Clive Court
Bartholomew's Walk
Cambridgeshire Business Park
Ely, Cambridgeshire
CB7 4EA
United Kingdom
www.itgovernance.co.uk

© Andrew Pattison 2025.

First published in the United Kingdom in 2025 by GRC Solutions.

ISBN 978-1-78778-589-2

Cover image originally sourced from Adobe Stock.

The author, who has dyslexia, used generative AI in the development of this book. AI-derived content was thoroughly reviewed, adapted and rephrased to better reflect the author's intent and to ensure factual accuracy.

ABOUT THE AUTHOR

Andrew Pattison is the Global Head of GRC and PCI Consultancy at IT Governance, a GRC Solutions company. With a career stretching back to the mid-1990s, Andrew has worked extensively in information security, risk management and business continuity. He is currently supporting several major international organisations implement robust governance and risk approaches for the use and development of AI. He holds an MSc in Information Systems Management, is a certified auditor, and is accredited with both CISM® and CRISC® certifications. Alongside his consultancy work, Andrew has delivered comprehensive training across multiple GRC disciplines, including DORA, NIS, NIST, ISO/IEC 27001, business continuity, CRISC and CISM.

CONTENTS

Contents

CHAPTER ONE: UNDERSTANDING AI AND ORGANISATIONAL RISK

Introduction: Why has this book been written?

I started in IT/ICT back in the early 1990s; since then, I have worked in many different environments and organisations. The common theme through most of these was security in its many forms, and how it was affected by new technology, although I was positioned more on the 'leading edge' than the 'bleeding edge'.

I have heard many things and seen many changes in the use of technology. In simple terms, when I started, the Internet did not really exist, so I have seen it all evolve. In my experience, new technology generally has a significant effect but not normally in the way experts predict.

There are a few people who do get it right – there is a great interview with David Bowie basically talking about the impact of social media, which was recorded long before it even existed:

"The actual context and the state of content is going to be so different to anything that we can really envisage at the moment, where the interplay between the user and the

> *provider will be so in simpatico it's going to crush our ideas of what mediums are all about."*[1]

We are in this space currently with artificial intelligence. Admittedly, this a term I really do not like – but then again, I don't like the term 'cyber security' either.

Very few subjects have had so much rubbish spouted about them. We are currently watching a dog chasing its own tail: a lot of the chatter around AI is marketing departments shouting at other marketing departments; every vendor feels they have to throw the term AI into their product description as no one will take them seriously if they do not.

Taking the above into consideration, we are, however, on the edge of a paradigm shift and the impact of AI is going to be as dramatic as the industrial revolution. What this will look like, however, I am not going to pretend to have the slightest idea.

What I do understand is that organisations must deal with this in a practical and sensible way. They need to understand the risks and opportunities, and manage these in a way that ensures the organisation delivers on its objectives while embracing the change to its best advantage.

This is the aim of this guide: to give order to the chaos that is being unleashed on the world.

---

[1] BBC, Newsnight, 1999, David Bowie speaks to Jeremy Paxman on BBC Newsnight (1999),
https://www.youtube.com/watch?v=FiK7s_0tGsg.

Just for the avoidance of doubt, I have used AI in creating this book. As a dyslexic (the cool term is neurodivergent), I am never short of ideas on many subjects but I struggle with structure and flow, and this is where AI can be very helpful.

I would, however, suggest that when using AI to support creating the written word, never assume it is correct. Remember the old saying "rubbish in and rubbish out" – this is even more relevant with AI. There are some major or potential problems with reliance on AI: do not assume it is correct and be wary of references or attributed sources of information.

In compiling this book, I think of Miles Kington's view on the difference between knowledge and wisdom: that knowledge is knowing that a tomato is a fruit and wisdom is knowing not to put it in a fruit salad.[2] This is what I find with AI, but note that this is not always the case.

The other issue is how AI writes. It's often not particularly good or, more to the point, a bit lacking in 'soul', so even though I will have processed paragraphs through the LLM several times, tweaking as I go, it still needs to go through an editor to make it more natural and acceptable to the reader.

So, it is useful, but as a rule, I probably disagree with the output of AI as much as 50% of the time, and it is probably completely wrong in at least 25% of what it produces. This

---

[2] In Morocco, not only will they put tomatoes in what is basically a fruit salad but they also add prawns and a dressing! It's absolutely fantastic, and here lies the problem with assumptions.

is not scientific in any way, of course, and is more my gut feeling on its accuracy and the quality of its output. AI is useful to a point, but you need to be careful.

To make sure your AI-derived content is correct, you first need to have the knowledge to ask the right question, and then you need the knowledge to know if the answer is correct. With that in place, it can be a very useful tool.

For those of you who want a more in-depth understanding of AI in all its manifestations, I highly recommend *Artificial Intelligence* by Dr Julie E. Mehan.[3]

Why AI and risk management matter

In very simple terms, risk is something that has the potential to stop an organisation reaching its objectives. From that perspective, it's not complicated, and risk management does not have to be complicated (although it often is). When we look at technology, risk can be a little more complicated than other areas, as we are quite often dealing with something that is difficult to quantify because it is new. The risk professional sometimes has to do a bit of 'crystal ball gazing', as we may be trying to quantify a risk in relation to technology that is new to us as well as changing the way organisations operate. This can make it very difficult to cover all the angles, so most of the time you base your view on past experiences and, not unusually,

---

[3] Julie Mehan, *Artificial Intelligence*, ITGP, 2024, *https://www.itgovernance.co.uk/shop/product/artificial-intelligence-ethical-social-and-security-impacts-for-the-present-and-the-future-second-edition*.

'gut feel' (this is where someone who is neurodiverse can be very useful).

AI risk matters because it is far more complex than, say, a normal information security risk assessment, which you might base on ISO 27005 (which is an international standard for assessing information security risks). When doing a risk assessment against these guidelines, the process is very straightforward and we are normally only really concerned with confidentiality, integrity and availability.

With AI risk, there are simply more variables and more complexity depending on what is being reviewed. Impact has far more complexity in the calculation, and as this is still a very new area, understanding the real-world impacts is a significant challenge.

For instance, we have a tendency to use the term 'AI', but this covers many areas, such as automation or the use of complex language models. When reviewing risk, these are different. As stated, we also need to consider the impact assessments that, again, make it more complex (similar to when doing business impact analysis or data privacy impact assessments).

This complexity means that we need to pay special attention to AI risk – it could encompass anything from a whole range of disciplines, and affect nearly any part of the organisation.

So, it matters because without a clear understanding of the associated risk of using AI, an organisation cannot make a reasoned decision on what it means to them.

Fundamentally, does taking this risk drive a definable and understandable benefit?

Defining risk in the age of AI

Risk management in the age of AI encompasses not only traditional concerns like financial, operational and cyber security threats, but also emerging challenges unique to AI technologies. This makes the process of looking at traditional impact areas such as confidentiality, integrity, availability and authenticity that much more complex and harder.

As AI systems increasingly influence decision-making across industries, new risks such as algorithmic bias, loss of privacy, lack of transparency and unintended consequences become significant.

When looking at risk, we must also consider the overuse of the term and the reality of the implementation and integration of AI into systems and services. We need to be sure we are not reacting to hot air but to reality. Furthermore, when looking at the risk, remember that you can only impact the things you can control. Avoid focusing on the areas that you have no control over as you cannot impact these.

Defining risk in this context requires an understanding of both the potential benefits and dangers of AI.

AI risk needs to be considered across and within the full system life cycle, and within the context of elements that further complicate the risk area, like Cloud, outsourcing and data portability.

This involves assessing the probability and impact of failures in AI deployment, whether they stem from flawed data, inadequate oversight, malicious misuse, or lack of competency in the development, implementation and use.

The GRC professional must also understand that AI risks now extend beyond organisational boundaries and traditional risk considerations. They affect broader issues that are often overlooked by businesses, including societal trust, ethics and equity.

Adopting a comprehensive approach to risk definition and management gives you a clearer view of the relationship between the AI tools you aim to use, the risks they present and your broader organisational objectives. Having a clear view of this means you can better balance innovation with responsibility, ensuring your AI use contributes positively to societal and organisational goals.

This isn't something you can implement after the fact, however. Organisations need to have a risk framework capable of dealing with this already in place to appropriately manage the challenges of AI risk.

The AI revolution: Opportunities and challenges for organisations

It's a common mistake to focus exclusively on risk when opportunities are of equal importance. What I mean by this is that we can sometimes only focus on risk when some risk conditions could, in specific circumstances, also represent an opportunity for the organisation.

A business can decide to do something even if it is considered a risk because it presents an opportunity. The governance, risk and compliance (GRC) function needs to ensure these opportunities are recognised, which is a major challenge. Too often, they can be seen as the 'computer says no' department.

On the flip side, the business needs to understand that we are not dealing with a zero-sum issue. It needs to understand what the risks are, work out the balance between risk and opportunity, and make the correct decision for the business and for those affected.

It is the business that makes the decision; the GRC or security practitioner's role is to ensure that the business understands the risk and makes an informed decision.

The ethical dimensions of AI

Understanding the ethical dimensions of AI is critical to ensuring that these technologies do not cause harm – intentionally or otherwise.

AI is not autonomous in the sense that we usually mean; in the general sense, it is driven or directed by human intelligence. It is not conscious. It cannot decide based on some understanding of itself or self-awareness. It has no sense of morality nor a moral compass. The only ethical framework to which it will adhere must be programmed into it.

As AI systems increasingly influence decisions in all areas of our lives, questions about fairness, accountability, transparency and privacy become even more important. This is especially true as our information – whether it be information about us or information we rely on to make our own decisions – becomes even more important.

There is already a significant deployment of AI (in its broadest scenes) in healthcare, and its ability to process huge amounts of clinical information (especially in digital imaging) is dramatic, but the human element is still incredibly important. Healthcare is potentially the area that AI will give the biggest and quickest impact, both for health organisations and the public at large.[4]

Ethical AI development means addressing biases in data and algorithms that could perpetuate or amplify societal inequalities. This may be more important to some organisations than others: your concern may simply be how you are using AI language models, for instance; or bias could be a central and important risk. Whatever value your organisation places on ethical development of AI, it needs to be reflected in your consideration and management of AI risk.

Respecting privacy and protecting sensitive data are essential in maintaining trust. There are particular issues around where data is stored and how that is used in learning models; these issues are especially important given the proliferation of free AI engines. It is always worth remembering that where something is free, you or your

---

[4] For examples, see: "Artificial intelligence in healthcare: transforming the practice of medicine" – PMC, *https://pmc.ncbi.nlm.nih.gov/articles/PMC8285156/*; "What Is The Impact Of Artificial Intelligence On The Healthcare Industry?", *https://www.forbes.com/councils/forbesbusinesscouncil/2023/11/06/what-is-the-impact-of-artificial-intelligence-on-the-healthcare-industry/*; "The Impact of AI", *https://digital-transformation.hee.nhs.uk/building-a-digital-workforce/dart-ed/horizon-scanning/ai-and-digital-healthcare-technologies/introduction/the-impact-of-ai*.

information is the product. This means that, before even developing a governance approach for AI, you need to establish your approach to security, privacy and information technology.

In its simple terms, you need to have defined goals and objectives, an implemented risk approach with assigned ownership, an agreed RACI (matrix that identifies those responsible, those accountable, those to be consulted and those to be informed), some form of agreement on actions, and a way to understand 'why' you are or are not doing something. Without these in place, the practical reality of using and developing AI in your organisation will bring into sharp focus your weaknesses in these areas.

Ethical considerations also extend to the potential displacement of jobs and the societal implications of autonomous systems, but this should not be overestimated or overly concerning. As has been shown throughout history when technology displaces humans due to cost or efficiency, humans go and do something else. Retraining and education will be important. For organisations, decisions more likely revolve around redeployment to existing or new roles. But, again, do not overestimate the cost that AI will remove from a business. Return on investment justification for 'paradigm shifts' should always be taken with a pinch of salt because they rarely approach what was expected.

The philosophical dimensions of AI

The philosophical implications of AI delve into the questions of what intelligence is, consciousness and the nature of human identity. These will be fundamental in the further development of AI, particularly when it is combined with quantum computing.

Quantum computing is still in its early stages, and is very much in its early stages of development. However, major companies with massive research budgets like IBM, Google and Microsoft are developing increasingly powerful and reliable systems.

This means that quantum computing is becoming a more viable technology and could have a dramatic impact on AI. This is unlikely to cause incremental change, but more fundamental.

While today's AI relies on classical computing infrastructure, the fusion of quantum mechanics with machine learning could lead to faster and dramatically more capable AI systems.

At the heart of AI lies a set of computationally intensive tasks: training deep learning models, optimising complex systems, and processing vast, high-dimensional datasets. These operations often stretch even the most powerful computers to their limits simply because the volume of data is so vast. Quantum computing offers a fundamentally different architecture: quantum bits (qubits), which can exist in multiple states simultaneously and influence each other through entanglement. Consider the difference in understanding of flight between the Wright Brothers and a NASA rocket scientist.

What quantum computing boils down to in relation to AI is that it could perform these intensive calculations exponentially faster than classical machines.

But even if this is the case, it's unlikely we'll have quantum computers replacing classical machines quickly – and AI that benefits from new quantum architecture isn't likely to be in our pockets or on our desks any time soon, but at some point they will be or will be accessing such devices.

In time, AI may challenge our understanding of what it means to 'think' and whether machines will be able to develop attributes and qualities like creativity, emotion or self-awareness.

These are a long way off. If you have seen much AI art, it is technically interesting but has no emotion or expression. It is very sterile in its production. AI is currently only able to mimic existing work, which means anything it produces is, at best, derivative, and at worst simple plagiarism. It also doesn't know what 'good' art (or writing) is, so human intervention is currently necessary to make AI output better than a functional average. This is why, when we see content produced by AI, it often seems like it was written by someone in marketing for a B2B company – because the Internet is awash with that content and, without further input, the AI will simply mimic what it sees.

Fundamentally, what we currently have isn't 'AI' as fiction would describe it. It's just very advanced algorithms that mimic intelligence.

AI can also pose a threat to human autonomy and agency, particularly as systems grow capable of making decisions that impact lives and societies. Traditionally, these sorts of decisions are made by the individual or by another person capable of examining the data necessary to make the decision. With the sheer processing ability of AI, it's able to analyse the same data and provide decisions based on its algorithms – but these decisions may not consistently match the decisions a human would make.

As stated earlier, we are on the edge of a paradigm shift that could fundamentally change aspects of our life. We will not know about this until it has happened. Imagine showing one of the Wright Brothers the 1949 Comet jet airliner, which was descended from the Wright Flyer just 43 years later.

Could we be in the same situation comparing the AI systems of 2025 with 2035 or 2045? It is difficult to tell. Technological change and speed are difficult to predict.

AI components

AI describes a wide range of tools and technologies that replicate or augment human cognitive functions, such as learning, reasoning and problem-solving. We are prone to using the term AI to describe the 'systems' or 'solutions' rather than their functions and complexity.

To give you a better understanding of AI, you need to understand its component parts and how they contribute to its function. The following are a high-level overview of these different types.

Machine learning (ML)

This may be considered what we mean by AI – the algorithms that enable digital devices to make and learn from decisions based on the data they have access to. This is not a new thing and has been around for a long time. It's used in everyday life in applications and services like Netflix; we interact with it on a daily basis even though we may not realise this is the case and may not consider it 'AI'. Its lack of transparency may cause issues as it becomes more pervasive.

Deep learning (DL)

This builds on ML and may be considered a subset. Deep learning leverages the power of the neural network and relies on multiple layers of abstraction to help the model learn complex patterns. This gives it the ability to analyse different factors[5] by extracting and combining features at various levels of abstraction, allowing the model to understand patterns, relationships and dependencies within the data.

One area where this is being used is medical imaging, where it is delivering significant benefits by analysing large amounts of data in real time and converting this into information that can then be evaluated by medical professionals.

Natural language processing (NLP)

This is the area of AI that has been creating the most noise over recent years, as it is the most visible development. Natural language processing allows digital devices to understand and interpret human language, translating the person's requests or requirements into queries that can be

---

[5] Factors could include: word meaning, grammar, sentiment, topic, context – the network learns increasingly abstract representations like 'positive review' or 'legal language'.

better understood by the AI, which can then respond in what is considered a useful manner.

Development

Another area that should be covered is where we are on the journey in AI. If you were to think of a clock that covers 12 hours, we are probably just past the first minute of the first hour on the journey. Broadly speaking, there are three stages on the AI journey.

Stage 1: Artificial narrow intelligence (ANI)

This is where we currently are. At this stage, AI is many things, but it's not intelligent. AI is performing specific and controlled tasks, which may be incredibly complex, but the AI is not going to start doing something else. If it's designed for autonomous car use, that's what it's going to do.

Stage 2: Artificial general intelligences (AGI)

At this stage, machines (or digital devices) are capable making decisions like humans (which also means potentially incorrect or illogical decisions). This would be based on the AI making connections across multiple domains and developing decisions based on generalisation; it will be both powerful and potentially disturbing.

Stage 3: Artificial super intelligence (ASI)

This is the 'Skynet' or 'Culture' level[6], where AI surpasses human abilities and capabilities. This is moving into the realms of science fiction. The level of computing power and energy consumption to achieve this will be off the scale. This is also referred to as 'the singularity' – a hypothetical point in time when artificial intelligence surpasses human intelligence, leading to rapid, uncontrollable and irreversible technological growth.[7]

We are currently at stage 1, and this is already having a fundamental impact – and it has for some time. The question is: when will we move to stage 2? Speculation points to anywhere between 2029 and 2060. For stage 3, it could be very quickly after stage 2. Ray Kurzweil, a leading futurist, predicts the singularity could occur around 2045.

Trends in AI technologies

Trends are difficult to consider when looking at AI. For most of 2024, there was a huge focus on and subsequent upheaval in the more creative areas, such as marketing and creative writing. Based on anecdotal evidence with organisations I have been working with, there seems to be a rollback on this as there is a realisation that creative

---

[6] Skynet is a reference to the Terminator film franchise, and Culture is a reference to the "minds" of the artificial intelligence at the centre of the books by Iain M Banks.

[7] The concept of the technological singularity was proposed by John von Neumann in the 1950s, when he referred to the idea of "ever-accelerating progress" leading to a point beyond which human affairs could not continue unchanged.

output from AI is a little generic, and this may be the case until we move into stage 2.

AI tools are very much going to accelerate certain activities and increase efficiency. AI is going to be very important to automation, where it can carry out specific tasks with more speed and efficiency than a human, but there will still need to be human interaction and oversight. For example, AI-generated code will need increased testing, but not by AI.

One area that has seen major developments is operational technology. There is a concerted effort to use AI for tasks like predictive maintenance, which AI is naturally good at. However, there are general issues in this as predictive maintenance uses both Cloud and wireless technologies, which are extremely problematic with OT, and, anecdotally, I have not seen evidence of it being used at scale in the wild.

Within the field of GRC, AI will not replace the GRC consultant or function, but it will make certain tasks quicker and more effective. The main reason 'we' will not be replaced is that GRC work is highly contextual: it relies a lot on interacting with people, and there are cultural aspects that are central to GRC. AI will certainly help speed up processes like policy and procedure creation and risk assessments, and will probably mean the GRC consultant can focus on areas where their experiences can drive real value.

AI technologies: Implications for neurodiversity

I may lack objectivity on this one as I am dyslexic, but in the future power struggle with our sentient machine overlords, it will be the neurodiverse among us who will be our last best hope for our survival. We will be saved due to my lack of understanding of what a semicolon is and what it does (I may have gone off on a tangent there).

The previous paragraph may feel flippant, but there are going to be real-world challenges where people who are neurodiverse will be better placed to deal with control or even counter AI as it develops and integrates into every aspect of our existence.

AI has brought about transformative changes in society, potentially with significant benefits for the neurodiverse. It is in the process of breaking the glass ceiling that many neurodiverse people encounter.

Neurodiversity, which includes conditions such as autism, ADHD and dyslexia, describes a spectrum of cognitive and behavioural traits that affect how people interact with the world and other people.

One of the most profound impacts of AI on neurodiverse people lies in accessibility.

AI-powered tools, such as speech-to-text applications, personalised learning platforms and adaptive technologies, can cater to unique communication styles and learning needs. For example, children with autism may benefit from AI-driven apps that help them navigate social interactions by recognising and interpreting facial expressions.

However, integrating AI into the lives of neurodiverse people is not without challenges. Ethical considerations regarding data privacy, algorithmic bias and the potential over-reliance on technology are paramount.

CHAPTER TWO: BUILDING A RISK-AWARE AI STRATEGY

AI potentially presents opportunities for organisations, but it also introduces a unique and complex set of risks. I use the word "potentially" because the organisation needs to effectively understand and manage the risks, otherwise it will not be able to take advantage of these transformative opportunities.

This means the organisation needs to take a strategic approach to dealing with it.

To navigate these challenges effectively, organisations must establish an AI risk management framework. This framework provides a structured approach to identifying, assessing, mitigating and monitoring risks associated with AI systems throughout their lifecycle.

This chapter explores the essential components and implementation strategies for an effective AI risk management framework.

1. Importance of an AI risk management framework

Integrating AI into organisational processes amplifies traditional risks while also introducing novel ones, such as algorithmic bias, data privacy concerns and system reliability issues. This means that you need a risk management framework built to address these risks. If you already have a framework in place for managing other risks, build on it – your experience with that framework is a distinct benefit.

The key and most important part of any risk framework is that it works for your organisation, which is why we see fewer mentions nowadays of best practices and more on guidance. Adapting your framework to address AI is, in essence, about evolution, not revolution.

An AI risk management framework should have four primary goals:

1. **Alignment**: AI systems align with organisational goals, ethical principles and regulatory requirements.
2. **Proactive risk mitigation**: Risks are identified and addressed early in the development and deployment process. This needs to be structured and the risk practitioner needs to be visible and accessible to assist in the process.
3. **Trust and accountability**: Interested parties, including customers, employees and regulators, trust the organisation's use of AI technologies because there is evidence that the organisation has addressed the risks that concern them.
4. **Resilience**: The organisation is prepared to respond effectively to unforeseen challenges or failures. This term is starting to be more common in the GRC and security environment. The aim is to develop resilient systems and services that can meet the challenges that modern organisations encounter.

2. Integrating AI into existing risk management practices

Integrating AI into existing risk management practices can enhance the organisation's capabilities to identify, assess and mitigate risks. But it can also seem counterintuitive – like the AI is checking its own homework, or that AI-inherent risks and flaws will become part of the process itself.

AI-powered tools can process vast amounts of data in real time, uncovering patterns and anomalies that may go unnoticed through traditional methods. For example, predictive analytics can help anticipate financial fraud, operational disruptions or cyber security threats, enabling pre-emptive action.

But it's crucial to remember that the AI capabilities need to be aligned with the risk framework's needs. There's no point implementing an AI function that looks for problems outside the scope of the organisation's needs, for instance. These technologies are best selected to augment rather than replace human judgment.

Organisations must also address AI-specific risks, such as algorithmic biases or system vulnerabilities, through robust governance and oversight. This will initially be difficult to implement, but over time it will become part of your established processes.

Crucially, AI risk management cannot be done without human involvement.

3. Core components of an AI risk management framework

An effective AI risk management framework comprises several key elements:

3.1 Governance and compliance

Governance structures and compliance mechanisms ensure accountability and adherence to legal and ethical standards, which is especially crucial where AI is concerned as it could otherwise be simultaneously a 'magic box' that no one understands and a tool for reducing human oversight.

Key to this should be an AI governance committee. This is a cross-functional team responsible for overseeing AI risk management activities. It does not need to be a standalone group or new group: if you're familiar with or run an ISO management system, it can be a management committee; if you have an IT steering committee, it can be that. The key thing is that somewhere in the organisation there is accountability for the deployment and use of AI. What works for your organisation is what is important.

Your AI governance committee should have two immediate concerns:

- **Regulatory compliance**: Adhering to privacy laws such as the GDPR and CCPA, or AI-specific regulations like the EU AI Act. Remember: you may not have laws in your specific jurisdiction, but you may be operating in areas that do and these need to be taken into consideration.

- **Ethical guidelines**: Establishing principles for responsible AI use, such as transparency, inclusivity and safety. Remember that ethics are different in different places; do not assume your ethical approach is relevant or appropriate everywhere.

4. Governance models for AI and risk

I know it's a common theme in this book, but use what you already have in place. If you are struggling to understand what and how to do this, consider reading through some of the ISO standards listed at the end of this book. NIST is also developing AI management standards and has guidance in this area.

For smaller organisations, simply remembering to keep asking 'why' will generally help develop your understanding and oversight. As long as you can get answers, you will be moving in the right direction.

4.1 Risk identification

Identifying risks requires a thorough understanding of AI technologies, their applications and their potential impacts. This is where you need to have the right people in the room who can clearly explain and understand the AI technologies, and should be able to help the risk practitioner identify risks. Key activities include:

- **Mapping the AI environment**: Documenting AI use cases (these need to be realistic), data sources, algorithms and decision-making processes.

- **Risk categories**: Classifying risks into categories such as operational, ethical, regulatory and reputational. If there is a corporate risk approach and impacts are defined, try to use them as it means you are closer to the business and how it understands risk.
- **Interested-party analysis**: Identifying who is affected by AI systems and understanding their concerns. Again, this needs to be controlled and relevant.

4.2 Risk assessment

Once risks are identified, they must be evaluated to prioritise mitigation efforts. Risk assessment involves:

- **Likelihood and impact analysis**: Estimating the probability of a risk occurring and its potential consequences. AI-specific impacts can be more complicated than those of more 'traditional' technologies.
- **Scenario analysis**: Explore 'what-if' scenarios to understand risk dynamics under different conditions and ask 'why' a lot. Scenarios help you explain the problem to the business, as it focuses on real-world impacts, the possibility of the organisation not achieving its objectives and the delivery of value.
- **Risk heatmaps**: A combination of quantitative and qualitative risk analysis that easily shows a

representation that the business can understand and use to prioritise risk mitigations.

If you already have a system in place – such as a risk framework for an ISO 27001 information security management system – use this, but ensure that you take into consideration the additional requirements of AI.

4.3 Risk mitigation

Like any other risk framework, mitigating AI risks is about implementing measures to reduce their likelihood or impact. This may be challenging due to AI being an emerging technology; traditional mitigation approaches may not be enough and there will be a need for increased oversight. Key strategies for mitigating AI risk include:

- **Bias mitigation**: Auditing and refining algorithms to eliminate biases and ensure fairness. You will likely need specialist help for this, which will be defined by the complexity of your environment.
- **Robustness testing**: Evaluating AI systems under extreme conditions to ensure reliability. This needs strong human input from competent resources.
- **Privacy protections**: Implementing data encryption, anonymisation and secure storage practices. If you have a data protection officer (DPO), they will need to be involved – they have the specialist skills, so use them.

- **Human oversight**: Embedding human-in-the-loop processes to validate AI-driven decisions. The requirement for highly skilled and experienced subject matter experts is paramount, as well as strong GRC knowledge to manage broader risks.

It's worth noting that, with the vast potential scope for AI systems, the range of possible mitigations is also enormous. The right mitigation will depend on your organisation, the function and complexity of the AI, the source of data, and so on. There is no fixed list of solutions.

4.4 Monitoring and reporting

Continuous monitoring is critical for detecting and addressing emerging risks, and ensuring that your risk treatments and mitigations are functioning correctly. Monitoring systems should:

- **Track performance metrics**: Evaluate AI system effectiveness and reliability, as well as the performance of risk mitigation measures. Ensure that you measure what *needs* to be measured, not what is *easy* to measure.
- **Detect anomalies**: Use logging and AI-driven tools to identify unusual behaviours or outputs in real time that can be followed up on by a human.
- **Report risks**: Maintain transparent reporting mechanisms to inform interested parties of risk-related

developments. Different types of reporting may need to be tailored to the audience you are informing.

4.5 Continual improvement

AI systems and their operating environments evolve, so the risk management framework also needs to be reviewed and revised to keep pace.

Continual improvement isn't about any one activity – incidents may inform changes, and you may or may not need to update policies or training programmes – it's about making changes based on what you have observed. And remember that a lack of data about something doesn't necessarily mean nothing is wrong – it can equally mean that you're looking at the wrong things.

The key to ensuring continual improvement is making sure you take in data from the right sources and take the time to review it.

5. Steps to implement an AI risk management framework

Step 1: Establish a risk management team

Form a cross-disciplinary team with expertise in AI technologies, risk management, legal compliance and, if possible, ethics.

This team will lead the design and implementation of the framework and should refer to the previous section of this book to ensure the core components are addressed.

Give serious consideration to who is part of the team. This should include not just the risk practitioner but also technical resources who understand the use of AI in the organisation. It is also crucial that there is input from the business. The exact make-up will again be driven by the complexity of the environment or the organisation. If risk is just being reviewed and compiled by the GRC function and the AI people in the organisation – or, as will no doubt happen, by asking an LLM what the risks are – then you are going to run into problems. It is essential that the business is involved as, in essence, they are business risks; this is a fundamental principle. Also ensure that you have people from different levels within the organisation – if you only have senior managers, you are just going to get a view from their specific vantage point. The 'shop floor' needs to be involved to get as full and rounded a view as possible.

Step 2: Define objectives and scope

Clearly articulate the goals of the risk management framework and define its scope, including the specific AI systems and processes it will cover. The scope should include any areas that you will be using or potentially using AI.

This is where the question of 'why' needs to be addressed. If the use of AI is not going to give any tangible benefit and drive value, it should not be used. 'Peer pressure' because other organisations are using it is not justification.

A further complication is that, as you start this process, you may find that the use of AI is already prevalent in your organisation. It may be already having impacts and, from an uncontrolled starting point, a lot of AI has been in use for years without being talked about.

Step 3: Develop policies and guidelines

Draft policies and guidelines that establish the principles and procedures for managing AI risks. These need to align with the organisation's values and legal requirements. Understand that these will evolve over time, and other policies, procedures and processes may need to be addressed and modified to address new challenges and changes.

Getting the policy correct is crucial: it's a key building block and needs to be a strong foundation. Remember that the policy defines the direction of travel, not how to get there. It should be straightforward, to the point and understandable – its key duty is to define the organisation's position so that anyone in the organisation can understand it. Detail should be addressed in the procedures and processes, not in policy.

Step 4: Implement risk tools and processes

Deploy tools for risk assessment, monitoring and reporting. Establish workflows for risk identification, escalation and resolution. If you already have a process that works, use that – make sure that all aspects of AI risk are considered, but try not to overcomplicate the issue. If you can, risk management is best implemented so that it's simple, consistent and repeatable.

There are multiple tools that deal with risk specifically in relation to security risk (CIA) that are based on the requirements of ISO 27005. There are few tools specifically designed around AI risk because the market is immature. This will change, however, as organisations implement risk based on either NIS guidelines or the ISO 42001 standard.

Step 5: Train staff and build risk awareness

Train employees and stakeholders on AI risks, the framework's objectives and their roles in risk management. Part of this is making sure everyone knows which tools and systems are AI – it may not be obvious, so it's crucial that each person understands this so they can identify and address any risks. Promote a culture of accountability and vigilance. This may be a legal requirement (such as under the EU AI Act), but regardless of the legal status, staff and stakeholders need to be informed to help them make sensible decisions.

Step 6: Risk assessments

Compile a comprehensive inventory of risks associated with AI initiatives. Engage with stakeholders across the organisation to capture diverse perspectives – if you have business input, you will have a far more accurate and comprehensive set of relevant risks.

A good place to start for AI risk is the OWASP Top 10 2025. These may not all be relevant and would need to be tailored and take into consideration your context as the risks[8] are

---

[8] LLMRisks Archive – OWASP GenAI Security Project, *https://genai.owasp.org/llm-top-10/*.

reasonably technical, but they are worth considering as a starting point. For instance, from the OWASP LLM risks:

1. Prompt injection
2. Sensitive information disclosure
3. Supply chain
4. Data and model poisoning
5. Improper output handling
6. Excessive agency
7. System prompt leakage
8. Vector and embedding weaknesses
9. Misinformation
10. Unbounded consumption

A more general view of risk can be summarised as follows (as described in a Forbes article[9]):

1. Lack of transparency
2. Bias and discrimination
3. Privacy concerns
4. Ethical dilemmas
5. Security risks
6. Concentration of power
7. Dependence on AI
8. Job displacement

---

[9] "The 15 Biggest Risks Of Artificial Intelligence", Forbes, *https://www.forbes.com/sites/bernardmarr/2023/06/02/the-15-biggest-risks-of-artificial-intelligence/*.

9. Economic inequality
10. Legal and regulatory challenges
11. AI arms race

Other risks that can be looked at as well could include:

1. Unintended consequences (positive and negative)
2. Return on investment (use of AI)
3. Reputational damage
4. Unapproved use of AI
5. Overselling the use of AI
6. Organisational morale (impact on)
7. Negative impact on ROI of current technology deployment

The above lists may be a useful place to start, but, as with all risk, it needs to be specific to your organisation. So, if you are considering deploying AI in your operational technology environment in an oil refinery or using it to draft letters in a hospital, the risks and impacts will be different.

This inventory should cover all areas where risks could materialise: projects, existing systems, supply chains, customers, etc. All areas within the scope need to be considered. Key to this is understanding what the organisation owns in terms of assets. Physical assets are straightforward to understand and identify, but data and information assets are more complex and diverse. At this point, you have to ask an important question, which must be honestly answered: "Do we know what data and

Information we own, and do we know where it all is?" If you're honest, the answer is probably 'no', and this is the first thing to address. After that, you need to understand what its value is and whether this accurately drives its classification. If your answer is 'no' to the first question, it's likely that 'no' is also the answer to the second question. This is exactly the same question we ask when looking at security: "What do you have and what is it worth?"

One of the areas where experienced GRC professionals will need to pay particular attention is assessing impact, as this is far more complex and nuanced than in a standard impact table. It is also an area where there is little historical quantitative data for review and guidance as to the real-world impacts of AI when it goes wrong. When looking at these, the following table would be a good place to start:

Table 1: Assessing Impact

Impact	Low	Medium	High
Fairness			
Accountability			
Transparency and explainability			
Security and privacy			
Health and safety			
Financial			
Accessibility			

Human rights			
Economic			
Access to financial or economic opportunities			
Environmental sustainability			
Governmental/political			
Cultural			

From the table above, an organisation would need to define impact severity if the scenario came to pass relative to their unique position and business. Be very cautious of supplied impact tables as they are very specific to an organisation – for example, impacts in relation to health and safety are going to look very different for a small accountancy firm compared to the operator of an oil refinery.

Impacts will also depend on the regulatory or legal framework an organisation operates in. For instance, specific outcomes could result in a huge fine in one regulatory area, but in another area that would not be the case. The impact for the same scenario can be very different.

Just to reiterate the importance of this question, understanding what you have is paramount – and lots of organisation do not know what they have – so a robust data classification and handling environment is essential. If you do not know what you have, you cannot protect it and you would also have no idea of the impact of AI on it.

Step 7: Review and refine

Once you have gone through the risk process, you can start to evaluate the effectiveness of the framework and make necessary adjustments to address evolving risks and organisational needs. Timescales for reviewing risk will be based on your organisation's needs.

At a minimum, you would review risks annually, but under some conditions you could be reviewing certain risks or types of risk and based on your context this could be on a daily or weekly basis.

CHAPTER THREE: IDENTIFYING AND ASSESSING RISKS

The evolving risk landscape

The risk landscape for organisations wishing to use AI is complex. It encompasses technical, operational, ethical, cultural and regulatory dimensions. AI may not even be something that an organisation has decided to or wishes to use, but is forced on them as it is built into a SaaS application that is central to their business operation. This means that all organisations – although similar – are inherently different.

These risk attributes are on top of the general business and security risks that need to be considered. Other forms of impact must also be considered, similar to the way that impact assessments are conducted for data protection or business continuity. Simply because something is not considered a risk to the organisation (or the risk is considered acceptable to the organisation) does not mean that the impact is never felt. AI can have immense consequences for other entities, including other organisations and the wider public.

In all aspects of GRC, the lack or the loss of control is incredibly dangerous. At its simplest, the aim of the GRC discipline is to create a controlled and consistent environment. AI may make these environments more complicated, unpredictable and fast changing.

Operationally, there are challenges in integrating AI systems with existing infrastructure, ensuring system reliability, and mitigating the potential for unintended consequences, such as automation failures or misinformation.

This integration is further complicated by the fact that the business wants to do this yesterday. One of the biggest risks we are facing is this feeling that an organisation *needs* to deploy AI, but when this is investigated further, the justifications are flimsy. The 'need' is likely led and driven by marketing in other organisations, compounded by the fear of being left behind.

Ethical risks arise from potential breaches of privacy, the perpetuation of discrimination, and the societal impact of AI deployments that prioritise efficiency over human welfare or, even worse, a misunderstanding of what the AI is doing with personal data. From a practical business point of view, the key risks are around privacy, as this is the most likely to result in significant regulatory fines and reputational damage.

Cultural risks are those that derive from how AI is perceived by people – both the wider public and employees. Where employees see AI as replacing human workers, for instance, there's a significant risk to organisational morale and the ability to retain talent. Wider society can also retaliate against businesses that seem to be 'on the side of the machines' by boycotting them or using competitors. Regulatory risks stem from evolving compliance requirements and legal uncertainties, as governments and international bodies strive to keep pace with AI's rapid development.

The European Union is trying to make sure it is the leader in this field, and because of its importance as an international market, organisations elsewhere in the world would be wise to keep the EU's regulatory requirements in mind.

Data risks: Privacy, security and integrity

AI systems rely heavily on vast amounts of data, making privacy, security and integrity critical concerns in their development and deployment.

Collecting and using sensitive personal information can expose individuals to privacy risks such as identity theft, surveillance and loss of autonomy if not properly safeguarded.

Organisations need to be very focused on this where they are in a heavily regulated environment. They also must be very honest about how effective they are at this.

Data breaches or unauthorised access can also compromise the security of AI systems, leading to significant financial, reputational and operational damage. This isn't just about configuring the AI system to minimise security risks, but also about wider security hygiene. After all, if a malicious actor gets hold of someone's credentials to access your network, the security measures applied to the AI itself may not even matter.

It's also essential to protect the integrity of data, because inaccurate, incomplete or biased datasets can lead to flawed AI outputs. Beyond simply weakening or ruining the results of processing, this can perpetuate inequities or cause unintended harm. This is the classic case of 'rubbish in, rubbish out' that applies to all processes.

Addressing these risks requires a robust approach to data governance, including applying relevant technical controls. Regular independent audits, which should be comprehensive and detailed, will be essential as the use of AI becomes more pervasive.

Transparent practices that ensure compliance with privacy laws and ethical standards may also be valuable for ensuring privacy protection and preserving the organisation's reputation. The need for this will continue to develop, and this space will come under more scrutiny and regulation as governments and regulators grapple with the problem of protecting individuals' data.

Algorithmic risks: Bias, transparency and accountability

"The blame for bias in AI is often laid on biased data used in training the AI. But the causes of biases go far deeper than that. Implicit bias can sneak into AI algorithms as a result of these real human tendencies."[10]

AI brings into sharper focus what bias is out there and how it affects decision making. As AI becomes more prevalent (and thus more likely to be feeding on the outputs of other AI systems), the risks posed by bias will become more of an issue. Furthermore, our attempts to counter it may just make it worse. This could end up being a circular, self-perpetuating problem that could significantly impact the ability of AI to do anything sensible.

---

[10] Dr Julie E. Mehan, *Artificial Intelligence – Ethical, social, and security impacts for the present and the future*, ITGP, 2024, chapter 5.

Bias in algorithms can arise from training data or assumptions in model design, leading to unfair or discriminatory outcomes. These can perpetuate societal inequalities or result in decisions that don't match what a neutral observer might expect (these are all, of course, based on value judgments). Understanding what data is used, how it is constructed and how bias might affect it is crucial, but this is complex and difficult to ascertain. It may also be further complicated if training data has itself been derived from AI.

Transparency is another critical challenge, as many AI models – particularly complex ones like deep learning systems – make it difficult to understand how decisions are made. This lack of explainability undermines trust and limits the user's ability to identify and address errors or biases. Organisations need to address this risk, which could be during design or procurement, as part of a service contract, etc.

Accountability is equally vital; as AI systems take on more decision-making roles, it becomes essential to determine who is accountable for these decisions and their outcomes. This could fall on the developers or operators, or at an organisational level. Fundamentally, accountability for these actions will rest with the organisation deploying the systems, and it needs to be able to justify any outcomes of AI-driven decisions.

Tackling these risks requires the organisation to adopt ethical design principles, rigorous testing and explainable AI frameworks to ensure that AI systems operate fairly, transparently and responsibly. This is a matter of risk, not just management. This is where governance models become more and more important, because this allows accountability to be asserted and the risks balanced against the organisation's objectives.

Operational risks: Deployment and maintenance of AI systems

Deploying and maintaining AI systems isn't just a matter of project management and day-to-day duties. AI systems pose significant operational risks.

While AI technologies may promise transformative capabilities, integrating them into existing workflows and systems is often complex and fraught with challenges. It is imperative that the organisation considers not just the opportunities posed, but also the risk.

Not fully understanding the impacts during deployment or inadequate maintenance can lead to system failures, inefficiencies or unintended consequences, which can undermine trust and cause financial or reputational harm.

Deployment challenges

Deploying AI systems requires a deep understanding of both the technology and the operational environment in which it will operate. This is always going to be a challenge as the subject is so large and evolving. A person cannot understand everything; they need a team with specific skill sets. It's no different from security, where there is a big difference in skills and knowledge between cyber ops and GRC – they are different disciplines.

Just like any other deployment, compatibility issues with legacy systems, inadequate infrastructure and poorly defined objectives can hinder the implementation. However, AI can also *accelerate* the speed of failure while leaving the organisation with less understanding of the cause. The more complicated the plumbing, the harder it is to find a leak.

One of my first jobs in IT was implementing stock control systems for plant nurseries. A common occurrence was that users believed it would solve their problems, but if they simply used it to replicate their existing approach, their system simply failed faster and more dramatically. AI is not going to solve all your problems: it's not a silver bullet and it's not a magic box.

Organisations must also navigate challenges such as training employees to work with AI tools without undermining the organisation, and managing resistance to change where people see threats to what they do and how they do it. We do not need to encourage a twenty-first-century version of the original saboteurs (who were reputed to throw their wooden shoes into machines to break them) or Luddites (who raided mills in England to destroy machines).

A poorly planned deployment may lead to AI models that perform suboptimally, fail to adapt to real-world conditions, or generate outputs that are inconsistent with business needs and unintended consequences.

One idea that organisations need to view with extreme caution is that deployment of AI will enable significant and quick reduction in head count. There is evidence that the rush to reduce head count in certain creative industries may be premature, which can make organisations vulnerable to unrealistic expectations.[11]

Don't believe the hype – understand the real capabilities!

Data dependence and scalability

AI systems are highly data-dependent, so their effectiveness hinges on the quality, volume and relevance of the data they process and significantly on the data that was used to learn.

During deployment, insufficient or unrepresentative data can result in models that fail to generalise to new scenarios. This isn't a failing unique to AI, but a lack of human involvement could mean that this goes unrecognised.

Scalability is another concern: AI systems that perform well in small-scale tests may encounter bottlenecks or inefficiencies when applied at an enterprise or global scale. There are additional unknowns as to how AI will perform at scale from a purely physical perspective due to its immense power usage. In the long term, can we – or the organisation – afford AI?[12]

---

[11] CREATe, "Is AI replacing creative work? New study finds complexity and continuities", October 2024, *https://www.create.ac.uk/blog/2024/10/31/is-ai-replacing-creative-work-new-study-finds-complexity-and-continuities/*.

[12] Lauren Leffer, "The AI Boom Could Use a Shocking Amount of Electricity", *Scientific American*, October 2023, *https://www.scientificamerican.com/article/the-ai-boom-could-use-a-shocking-amount-of-electricity/*.

AI's energy footprint may mean that 'true AI' is only accessible to mega corporations and governments. This means that the organisation should be prepared to encounter a limit to the scalability of its AI systems.

Ensuring future access to data pipelines, storage and computational resources that can support AI operations may be a challenge.

Maintenance and monitoring risks

Once deployed, AI systems require ongoing maintenance to remain effective and secure. This is true of any system, but it is amplified for AI due to its additional functionality and speed, so regular human interaction is essential.

Regular updates and retraining are necessary to keep AI systems aligned with evolving conditions and objectives.

Additionally, AI systems are susceptible to adversarial attacks, where bad actors intentionally manipulate inputs to exploit vulnerabilities. One of the key areas is that AI will be susceptible to the 'poisoning' of its data sources – this may be one of the most effective ways to destabilise and reduce the effectiveness of AI.

Continuous monitoring and robust information security (reference to information security is intentional) measures are essential to mitigate these threats.

Mitigating operational risks

In a nutshell, organisations should implement an artificial intelligence management system (AIMS). If you already have formal management systems in place (such as a quality management system or an information security management system), you can integrate the AIMS into your current governance approach.

It is essential that, as part of this management system, organisations have an effective and efficient risk process that is meaningful, implemented and live. Due to the nature of AI, simply going through the motions with risk management (and unfortunately this is more prevalent than you think, even with ISO certified organisations) is no longer an option as the game is changing and misunderstanding of the risk and lack of mitigation could be catastrophic.

As part of this, it is essential to implement the following:

- A proactive and structured approach to AI deployment and maintenance.
- Thorough planning, stakeholder engagement and rigorous testing under diverse conditions.
- Clear protocols for monitoring and updating AI systems, as well as investing in tools for explainability and risk management.
- Treating AI as a dynamic component of operations rather than a one-time implementation.

While AI systems hold immense potential, their deployment and maintenance are accompanied by significant operational risks. It's critical to recognise and address these challenges early – this isn't just about managing the risk, but also about seizing the opportunities.

This will undoubtedly be a challenge for many security (information and cyber), audit and GRC functions, who will also likely find their roles emphasised as AI develops and becomes more pervasive.

Mitigating external risks

While AI offers transformative potential, its external risks cannot be ignored and need to be taken seriously. It is essential to ensure transparency and inclusivity in AI development processes. While it isn't always possible to engage with external parties at all stages, engaging with diverse stakeholders (both internal and external, where possible) can help identify risks early to anticipate and mitigate social impacts.

Transparency may be more difficult for some organisations than others, and it would be wise not to underestimate the cultural and structural challenges of implementing transparent processes in any meaningful sense.

Collaborating with interested parties can be beneficial, particularly for both suppliers and customers, and this can help shape your practices.

External risks: Regulatory, social and environmental impacts

Adopting AI technologies is accompanied by external risks that include regulatory, social and environmental concerns.

These risks reflect the broader implications of AI systems on society and the planet, requiring organisations to address them thoughtfully to avoid unintended harm and maintain public trust.

Regulatory risks

The rapidly evolving regulatory landscape presents significant challenges for organisations deploying AI. Governments and international bodies are introducing laws and standards to address issues like data privacy, algorithmic bias and transparency.

Non-compliance with these regulations can result in legal penalties, financial losses and reputational damage. For instance, regulations such as the EU's General Data Protection Regulation (GDPR) impose strict requirements on data collection and processing, including specific conditions around automated decision-making, which clearly applies to the use of AI.

Current regulatory situation

International frameworks

- **Framework Convention on Artificial Intelligence**[13]: In September 2024, the Council of Europe opened for signature the first legally binding treaty on AI, focusing on aligning AI systems with human rights, democracy and the rule of law.

---

[13] Council of Europe, *Framework Convention on Artificial Intelligence and Human Rights, Democracy and the Rule of Law,* September 2024, *https://www.coe.int/en/web/artificial-intelligence/the-framework-convention-on-artificial-intelligence*.

Signatories at launch included the United States, the United Kingdom, the European Union, and others.[14]

- **Global Partnership on Artificial Intelligence (GPAI)/OECD.AI**: These two frameworks merged in 2024, and track state-level AI policies and initiatives in 71 countries and territories.[15]

Regional and national regulations

- **European Union (EU): AI Act[16]**: The EU's comprehensive AI Act, which came into effect in 2024, classifies AI systems based on risk and imposes strict requirements on high-risk applications, including transparency and data governance obligations.

- **China: Model Artificial Intelligence Law (MAIL) v.2.0[17]**: As of April 2024, China updated its AI regulatory framework to emphasise data localisation and sovereignty over data processing. It also sets out strict compliance requirements for AI systems operating within China's jurisdiction.

---

[14] Emma Roth, "US, EU, UK, and others sign legally enforceable AI treaty", The Verge, September 2024, *https://www.theverge.com/2024/9/5/24236980/us-signs-legally-enforceable-ai-treaty*.

[15] *https://oecd.ai/en/*.

[16] *https://eur-lex.europa.eu/eli/reg/2024/1689/oj/eng*.

[17] *https://zenodo.org/records/10974163*.

- **United Kingdom (UK)**: **AI Regulation White Paper**[18]: Published in August 2023, the UK's white paper outlines a pro-innovation approach to AI regulation, focusing on context-specific guidelines rather than a single comprehensive law. However, this was developed under the previous government, so the eventual objectives for regulation may differ.

Industry commitments and guidelines

- **Bletchley Declaration**: In November 2023, 28 countries, including the US, China and EU member states, issued a declaration emphasising international cooperation to manage AI risks and promote safe development practices.[19]
- **Frontier AI Safety Commitments**: In May 2024, major AI tech companies agreed to a set of safety

---

[18] *https://www.gov.uk/government/publications/ai-regulation-a-pro-innovation-approach/white-paper.*

[19] "The Bletchley Declaration by Countries Attending the AI Safety Summit", AI Safety Summit, November 2023, *https://www.gov.uk/government/publications/ai-safety-summit-2023-the-bletchley-declaration/the-bletchley-declaration-by-countries-attending-the-ai-safety-summit-1-2-november-2023.*

commitments during the AI Seoul Summit, focusing on responsible AI development and deployment.[20]

Social impacts and risks

We've already looked at some of the internal social risks and impacts, which primarily relate to risks associated with bias and inequality, and external risks are essentially extensions of these same risks, alongside the impact of automation.

As external risks, these manifest as changes in employment and training requirements, as well as impacts on public trust.

The increasing automation of tasks risks workforce displacement, particularly in organisations that rely heavily on repetitive or manual labour. This requires organisations to invest in reskilling programmes and to ensure current employees cannot be lured to roles in other organisations offering those opportunities.

Additionally, untreated bias and the misuse of AI in areas like surveillance or misinformation can erode public trust, prompting calls for greater oversight and transparency.

Environmental impacts of AI

It's well known that AI systems, particularly large-scale models, have a significant environmental footprint. There

---

[20] "Frontier AI Safety Commitments", AI Seoul Summit, May 2024, *https://www.gov.uk/government/publications/frontier-ai-safety-commitments-ai-seoul-summit-2024/frontier-ai-safety-commitments-ai-seoul-summit-2024.*

are memes about drying up lakes just to create images of cats.

Training and running advanced AI models require substantial computing resources, which consume significant amounts of energy. This may contribute to greenhouse-gas emissions and exacerbate global climate change. The environmental impact is further compounded by the growing demand for hardware and infrastructure to support AI operations.

However, applying AI where decision-making could be more effective and efficient could counteract the considerable resource cost. How this pans out will have a significant impact on the use and development of AI.

For instance, better initial diagnosis of medical scanning could reduce the requirement for additional scans or more specific scans, not only saving time and resources but also improving patient outcomes.

For example, in 2016, the NHS was spending at least £1.4 billion per year on chemotherapy.[21] If AI was able to reduce chemotherapy treatments by 50% due to more effective targeted treatment (this is the current direction of travel), this could result in savings of around £750 million, as well as increasing the number of patients able to go through chemotherapy treatment cycles and reducing such waiting lists.

---

[21] NHS England, "Chemo drug optimisation to improve patient experience of cancer treatment", May 2016, *https://www.england.nhs.uk/2016/05/chemo-drug-optimisation/*.

Similar decision-making processes in other organisations and settings can mitigate the overall environmental cost, despite the relatively high per-use cost for AI.

Having said this, organisations should prioritise energy-efficient AI solutions and understand the environmental impacts, explore renewable energy sources, and adopt practices such as system optimisation to reduce their energy consumption.

CHAPTER FOUR: DEVELOPING AN AI MANAGEMENT SYSTEM

So far, we've talked primarily about AI risk, including strategies and frameworks for managing that risk. What we need to look at now is how this can be addressed as a more joined-up part of the organisation. A risk regime doesn't stand alone, after all: it should be part of a larger organisational structure to not only manage the risk but also take advantage of opportunities, streamline processes and press towards business objectives.

This is what we mean when we talk about a management system.

There are sources of frameworks and standards available for developing management systems. Some of these are competing in approach, some are complementary, but all follow a set of basic principles and requirements. They may describe things differently and have different language – some talk about 'safeguards' while others talk about 'controls' – but there are only so many ways to describe essential facts of management, like needing a defined RACI.[22]

In my long career, I have used many different frameworks and approaches from many different sources. I gravitate

---

[22] A matrix that sets out those who are Responsible, Accountable, Consulted and Informed.

towards using frameworks and guidance from the following three:

1. International Organization for Standardization (ISO).
2. National Institute for Standards and Technology (NIST).
3. ISACA (originally the Information Systems Audit and Control Association).

My main source of approach (you could say world view) is ISO.

There are many reasons, not least I have been using ISO standards since the mid-1990s. I also come from an information security background and have been using ISO 27001 since its origination in the mid-2000s, as well as ISO 22301.

I like the ISO approach as it is heavily tailored to the organisation you're working with. Lots of people – even professionals in the space – consider it very prescriptive and restrictive, which it is not: ISO tells you *where* to get to, not necessary *how* to get there.

Fundamental to its outlook is that it is size, type and sector agnostic. ISO 42001 – the ISO standard for AI management systems – follows this principle, which ensures it is usable and scalable for small and medium-sized organisations that may be struggling to understand where to start with their AI governance approach. The Standard and supporting documentation give you the structure to deal with it in line with your organisation's needs and resources.

There are two other critical advantages of the ISO approach.

First is the structure of the management system, which follows a common approach and structure across all ISO management system standards. This means you can have an integrated system for multiple disciplines (such as information security, business continuity, quality, environmental management, etc.), which makes life a lot more straightforward and helps the organisation take advantage of efficiency savings. This also means that if you have certification for ISO 27001, you can integrate the requirements of ISO 42001 into your existing management system, removing duplication of certain key processes.

Second is its approach to risk. It uses ISO 31000 as a base standard/guidance, which informs the approach to both ISO 27005 (information security risk management) and ISO 23894 (AI risk management).

The approach I suggest in this book is based on ISO. I'm confident that, if implemented correctly and in the 'spirit' of the standards and guidance, you will be able to develop an effective AIMS that helps you meet your AI objectives and delivers value to the organisation.

Developing an AIMS is essential to ensure that AI is implemented responsibly, effectively and sustainably.

The management system allows us to frame our response to one very simple question, which should drive all our decisions on how we use, implement and manage AI: 'Why?' If the answer is 'to help reach organisational objectives and drive value', then use AI; if it is not for that reason, then don't – and specifically do not bend to peer pressure. Do not be driven by the noise and the desire to embrace anything that is new. If it does not drive value, do not do it. A management system helps ensure it drives value.

This chapter explores the key components, principles and practices necessary to establish a robust AIMS.

1. The importance of an AI management system

An AIMS serves as the foundation for governing AI projects and ensuring they align with organisational objectives, ethical considerations (more on ethics later) and regulatory requirements. It will enable the organisation to develop its use of AI in a controlled manner and ensure that it delivers the benefits, although you could argue that some of these current benefits are a little inflated by overactive marketing departments.

Unlike traditional management systems, an AIMS must account for the complexity and unpredictability of AI technologies, including their reliance on data, machine learning models and dynamic decision-making processes. So, although potentially adding more complexity to the organisation, the management system will help you frame and quantify how AI systems are designed, developed, implemented and used.

A well-designed, implemented and maintained system will mitigate risks, build stakeholder trust and ensure the long-term success of AI initiatives.

2. Key components of an AI management system

2.1 Governance framework

A governance framework establishes roles, responsibilities and decision-making authority for AI projects. It ensures accountability at every level, from data collection to model deployment. Having a number of defined standalone committees may not make sense for all organisations, but it is important that committees exist as a structural approach to help the organisation understand both its obligations and its actions to meet them. The key thing to remember with the governance framework is that it should give you the tools to understand and justify decisions. This has always been important for security and business continuity; it is even more important in dealing with AI because of the impact and speed of technology change.

Key elements include:

- **AI ethics committee**: A cross-functional team that oversees ethical considerations and ensures alignment with organisational values. This does not need to be a standalone function – it can be part of some other group or committee. If your organisation is developing AI products, it will be more active; if you are simply approving third-party products for use, its scope and activity will be reduced.
- **Policies**: Documentation outlining the acceptable use of AI, data privacy standards and risk management protocols. This also needs to be based on need and understanding of the risks and opportunities. When

developing policies, do not be fixated on best practices: understand what guidance is out there and use this to develop what works best for your organisation, addresses risk and delivers value.

- **Escalation mechanisms**: Processes for addressing issues, such as algorithmic bias or data breaches, in a timely manner. Again, this should be based on what works for your organisation.

At this level, you should also be defining objectives for the management system. This should be the duty of top management, which will be represented on the governance committee or equivalent body. In general, the objectives are likely to look something like the following, but with variations to match your organisation's needs and aspirations:

- Align AI projects with organisational strategy.
- Promote value generation.
- Promote ethical and responsible AI use.
- Ensure compliance with regulatory and industry standards.
- Monitor and mitigate risks throughout the AI lifecycle.
- Drive continual improvement and innovation.

2.2 Risk management protocols

Risk management is critical to the safe and effective deployment of AI systems. All organisations should be dealing with risk in a systematic and reliable way, and as we move into the AI arena, organisations need to be very honest with themselves about how they deal with risk. If you're doing a box-ticking exercise, this is going to be brought into sharp focus, so in most cases you will need to improve your risk approach. This will require investment and training, and an increase in levels of competence.

Features of an effective risk management regime were discussed earlier, but as part of an ISO-style management system, it's worth discussing in more detail.

To help develop the approach to risk management, first become familiar with the approach of ISO 31000 and then the detail of ISO 23894.

ISO 31000 is the specification for risk management as a general discipline. It sets out the key stages and elements, and provides guidance on how to take a risk that you may not properly understand and turn that into a set of actions to manage a risk that you now understand in relation to the business. ISO also produces topic-specific guidance based on ISO 31000, such as ISO 27005, which addresses information security risk management.

Even if you are familiar with ISO 31000 and ISO 27005, you will need to get to grips with ISO 23894, which is specific to AI risk management; AI risk is more involved than you might expect based on ISO 27005.

There are other approaches – for example, from NIST – and I am in no way dismissing them, but going the ISO route based on ISO 31000 means that a lot of organisations are using this as the base 'DNA' for their risk approach across many disciplines. This means there is a common language and basis for understanding, which has the advantage of talking in terms and language that the business understands and enables it to understand what you are talking about. This is incredibly valuable.

2.3 Data governance

AI systems are highly dependent on the quality and integrity of the data they consume. This means that effective data governance is essential, and needs to include:

- Data quality standards that ensure data used for training and decision-making is accurate, complete and representative;
- Adherence to data privacy regulations and applying protections to sensitive information;
- A strong understanding of where the data resides; and
- Methods for documenting data provenance and transformation of data to maintain transparency and traceability.[23]

2.4 Model development and validation

Building robust AI models requires stringent development and validation processes.

---

[23] If you're using an LLM, try starting a discussion with the AI on this subject. It's fascinating.

Development guidelines should identify best practices for designing, testing and refining AI models. NIST, ISO and the NCSC are good sources for this type of information.

AI models should be rigorously evaluated through validation and testing, including stress testing under edge cases. When testing, it's important that there is a strong human element. It would be problematic if there was an over-reliance on using AI for testing AI models; there should be a balance.

AI models should also be subject to explainability standards. These ensure that models provide interpretable outputs, which support transparency and accountability.

These are new disciplines, and many organisations will not yet have the expertise to implement and manage them.

2.5 Continuous monitoring and feedback

AI systems must evolve (and they will, faster than you can imagine) to remain effective in dynamic environments. The environment in which they operate will also evolve, and a combination of both could lead to inefficiencies or risks. As such, it's necessary to monitor AI systems and develop feedback processes.

Track KPIs to evaluate the effectiveness and efficiency of both the AI and the measures to control AI risk. Key risk indicators (KRIs) are also essential so that there are early warning mechanisms in place to identify potential issues and problems before they occur.

Use tools to detect anomalies early – these could even be AI-driven tools with humans alerted when anomalies are detected. These tools should be deployed to identify unusual patterns or system failures in real time.

Collect user and stakeholder input to refine and improve AI systems over time. This can be combined with data derived from other monitoring to help inform improvements.

2.6 Training and education

Building organisational capacity for managing AI requires ongoing training and education – this cannot be underestimated or overstated. This must be at all levels in the organisation. If you are based in the EU or your AI products are used in the EU, you are subject to the EU's AI Act which requires an AI awareness programme. Organisations will need to be creative in how this is delivered, as the depth of content will likely need to be tailored based on role, responsibility and access to AI systems. In many ways, it should reflect your RACI matrix.

Train employees in AI fundamentals, data literacy and ethical considerations as relevant to their roles and interaction with AI systems. AI fundamentals will look very different depending on the audience. If you are an AI developer, this will need to cover a broader set of concepts and in more detail than it would for an administrative assistant who may have access to an LLM to help them draft letters.

Promote understanding of AI-related risks and opportunities across all levels of the organisation. You can build on training programmes and use whatever delivery channels you already have.

Conduct workshops to simulate potential challenges and develop proactive solutions. This will help the organisation build both a strong understanding of AI functions and objectives, and expertise in responding to potentially challenging situations.

3. Principles of effective AI management

To ensure the success of an AI management system, organisations need to adhere to key guiding principles and approaches. When starting your AI journey, do not underestimate the challenge of achieving these. It's not sufficient to say you do this – you have to do it. This is very much a case of following the spirt of the law, not just the letter of the law.

3.1 Transparency

If you are using AI in any part of a process, you need to be upfront about this. Where this is particularly difficult is if AI is in your supply chain and you need to understand what impacts it has on what you are trying to achieve.

Taking this into consideration, AI systems must be transparent in their design, functionality and decision-making processes at all stages, no matter know trivial it may be. Openness and transparency are required to help foster trust with your stakeholders.

3.2 Accountability

Clear lines of accountability must be established to ensure that individuals and teams take responsibility for the outcomes of AI projects. As much as a conversation with

ChatGPT might feel like you're talking to a person, an AI system is not a person and cannot be accountable for its decisions.

In defining accountability, it's important to understand the impacts, and to recognise the requirements of the rest of the RACI, as accountability does not function without an understanding of these relationships.

3.3 Flexibility

AI management systems must be able to adapt to evolving technologies, regulations and organisational needs. To ensure flexibility and agility, good governance and a clear strategy are necessary. Without these in place, flexibility vanishes.

Flexibility enables organisations to remain competitive in a rapidly changing landscape, while governance brings a sense of control and calm. Ungoverned flexibility opens the organisation to a whole host of risks.

3.4 Ethical responsibility

Ethical considerations should guide every stage of AI development and deployment. Organisations must prioritise fairness, inclusivity and the well-being of all stakeholders. This is a challenge and will take time to develop and understand.

This can be widened to include bias. This is a complicated topic as all decisions made by anything with intelligence has a certain level of bias. Bias is key to intelligent beings surviving – it's what stopped us all being eaten by sabre tooth tigers 10,000 years ago.

In the long term, the effects of bias or countering bias (which means using bias) may make certain aspects of AI unworkable as we end up in the situation like a dog chasing its own tail. Its impacts will be more dramatic as we move into stage 2 of AI's development.

3.5 Collaboration

Effective AI management requires collaboration across departments, including IT, legal, compliance and business units. The governance function can drive the framework, but skilled project management resources are essential. The more one delves into AI, the more complex it becomes – for example, due to the potential implications for privacy, the involvement of a privacy and data protection specialist may be key.

This sounds easy and straightforward, but it is complex and difficult to deal with, particularly in large and complex organisations. It needs leadership at a senior level to ensure this happens and is effective. This is where an organisation – and particularly larger ones – should consider a dedicated leadership role, such as a chief artificial intelligence officer (CAIO).

4. Steps to implement an AI management system

Implementing an AIMS requires a structured approach as with any management system. When doing this, you are likely to get pushback – people will say this removes agility and flexibility. The counter to this is that, of all the areas that need a management system, it's crucial for AI, because if you get AI wrong, the implications could be catastrophic.

Step 1: Define objectives and scope

Identify the specific goals and scope of your AI initiatives, including the key areas where AI will be applied and the desired outcomes.

When doing this, it is always worth understanding why you are doing something – this will help you identify your objectives and the natural extent of the scope.

Step 2: Establish governance

Set up the governance framework, including roles, responsibilities and ethical oversight mechanisms. This needs senior leadership buy-in to be effective.

Step 3: Conduct a risk assessment

Evaluate risks and develop strategies to mitigate them. Use tools like risk heatmaps and scenario analysis to prioritise high-risk areas.

Step 4: Develop policies and procedures

Document policies and standard operating procedures for managing AI projects, including data handling, model validation and compliance checks. Ensure that all processes and procedures make it clear and understood who is responsible for each stage.

Step 5: Build capabilities

Invest in training, hiring and upskilling to build the expertise needed to manage AI effectively.

This needs to be a deep and extensive programme taking into consideration that the content will need to evolve over time as issues develop and change.

Step 6: Deploy and monitor

Roll out AI systems in phases, starting with pilot projects. Use monitoring tools to track performance and detect issues in real time. Increased overview during deployment is critical to ensure actions and events are what is expected, and results are not erroneous.

Step 7: Review and improve

Regularly review the AIMS and update it to address emerging challenges and opportunities. Deploying a Plan-Do-Check-Act approach is invaluable in achieving this.

CHAPTER FIVE: THE FUTURE OF AI AND RISK

Anticipating emerging risks in AI evolution

We may as well buy a crystal ball to see where AI is going. Anticipating emerging risks in AI evolution requires a forward-looking approach that combines technological foresight, ethical consideration and proactive governance.

All this will require significant investment in both people and resources, but it may well be essential for organisations that are using AI in a significant manner.

As AI systems become more autonomous and integrated into critical functions, risks include the development of unforeseen vulnerabilities. We already see vulnerabilities that can lead to adversarial attacks, misuse of generative AI for disinformation and the amplification of systemic inequalities, but future vulnerabilities could be exploited for completely different ends.

Emerging technologies like artificial general intelligence (AGI) will pose additional uncertainties, including challenges in maintaining control over increasingly sophisticated systems.

Collaboration between policymakers, technologists and ethicists is essential to establish adaptive regulatory frameworks and guidelines that evolve alongside AI capabilities. This will be further complicated with different regulatory approaches, such as those between the US and the European Union, and many US regulations being state-driven and not federal.

Robust testing, ethical safeguards and transparency can mitigate risks while fostering innovation. By anticipating and addressing these challenges, organisations can navigate the evolving AI landscape responsibly and sustainably.

The role of human oversight in AI systems

Human oversight plays a critical role in the development, deployment and management of AI systems. Central to this is good governance, and the requirement will only increase as the technology develops.

While AI can process vast amounts of data and perform complex tasks with remarkable efficiency, it lacks the capacity for moral judgment, contextual understanding and empathy – qualities intrinsic to human decision-making. The main issue with this is the perception that AI can do this – or that these things interfere with 'truly logical and rational' decision-making – which means that significant education is required at all levels to mitigate this very real problem.

Oversight also fosters accountability, as humans remain ultimately responsible for the outcomes of AI applications. Organisations at a senior level need to understand they are accountable – this means not just paying lip service to accountability, but taking real ownership of the use of AI within the organisation.

The big challenge for human interaction with AI will be as it moves into stage 2. By stage 3, AI will be potentially moving so fast that human intervention may be impossible – but, as mentioned earlier, that's a few years away and is in the arena of pure speculation.

Adapting to rapid changes in AI and regulations

Adapting to the rapid advancements in AI and the evolving regulatory landscape requires agility, foresight and a proactive approach – really, it needs 'controlled flexibility'.

As AI technologies continue to transform industries and everyday life, regulations will move to adapt and manage the change. The organisation must always keep in clear focus that the use of AI delivers benefits and value, and the regulatory environment will impact this significantly.

This is no small challenge – think about the journey that organisations have been on in relation to data protection and resilience (such as under the GDPR, NIS/NIS 2[24] and DORA[25]). It's not easy if you are impacted by these, but AI is a multiplier in the level of complexity: it may solve some problems but will cause others.

To manage risks related to regulatory compliance, the organisation needs to ensure that regulation is never a surprise. It typically goes through multiple stages, including public consultation, and is released with scheduled enforcement. Any basic compliance function should be able to keep pace with regulation.

However, matching this pace with the AI systems that the regulations are trying to control may be more problematic.

---

[24] Directive on network and information systems – a pair of directives from the EU directing member states to ensure that their critical infrastructure is resilient to cyber attacks and similar threats.

[25] Digital Operational Resilience Act – an EU law setting out requirements for the financial sector to manage operational risks, including within the supply chain.

A solution to manage one regulation may no longer function when the AI evolves or is replaced by the next iteration. As such, it's likely to be useful to design measures that are forward-thinking and future-proof.

Building resilient AI-powered organisations

Building resilient AI-powered organisations requires a strategic blend of technological innovation, robust infrastructure and adaptive leadership. Crucially, this must be built on awareness of the uses and limitations of the technology within the organisation.

Resilience in this context means the ability to leverage AI effectively while anticipating and mitigating potential disruptions, whether technical, ethical or regulatory. Organisations must invest in scalable and secure AI systems that can evolve with changing demands and technologies.

Equally important is fostering a culture of adaptability and ethical awareness among employees, encouraging staff to actively engage with and use AI-driven insights.

CONCLUSION

Embracing AI responsibly: A path to sustainable innovation

The rapid advancement of AI presents an unprecedented opportunity for innovation across industries, but its transformative potential must be approached responsibly. This requires the organisation to take ethical considerations, environmental sustainability and societal well-being into account at every stage of AI development and deployment, and ensure these standards are maintained as AI evolves.

This ensures that AI technologies not only drive progress but also align with the long-term objectives of the organisation.

The importance of ethical AI

Ethics is central to the responsible adoption of AI. Algorithms must be designed to operate fairly, transparently and inclusively, avoiding biases that could perpetuate discrimination or inequality. The problem with 'ethics' is that it is subjective and based on societal norms. Its subjectivity means that we work on the principle that our ethical view is correct and is what AI ethics should be based on. This is problematic and will create bias in the development of AI.

An unbiased AI system won't naturally evolve or miraculously appear. AI is not going to make inherently unbiased and fair decisions. The organisation's governance framework needs to take this into account.

For example, systems that handle sensitive tasks, such as hiring, lending or medical diagnostics, should be subject to rigorous human oversight to ensure impartiality and reliability. How this is practically achieved needs to be developed and will in itself create a new discipline in relation to GRC.

Environmental sustainability in AI

Sustainability is a critical dimension of responsible AI adoption. Large-scale AI models consume enormous energy, which contributes to carbon emissions and resource depletion. Organisations must prioritise energy-efficient practices, such as optimising algorithms and adopting renewable energy sources for data centres. The organisation should also consider how it can best balance its efficiency gains against the resource cost.

By addressing the environmental footprint of AI, businesses can contribute to global climate goals while enhancing productivity.

The vast resources required to run and develop AI may be the limiting factor in how it is used and deployed. It may result in more advanced AI systems being limited to specialist and specific areas that can justify the resource cost and responsibly manage how much they are used. Resources will always be finite, and this needs to be factored in as the technology develops.

Governance and accountability

Organisations should establish clear policies and processes for monitoring AI systems, addressing risks, and responding to ethical or operational challenges.

Regular audits, engaging with interested parties and adhering to regulatory standards can help organisations stay accountable and compliant. Moreover, fostering a culture of responsibility within teams through training and awareness initiatives empowers employees to consider the broader implications of their AI projects – and will be the best way to ensure their success.

Innovation through governance

Far from being a constraint, governance is an enabler of sustainable innovation (so we can deliver value).

Organisations that proactively address ethical, environmental and societal considerations can differentiate themselves in a competitive landscape, attract conscientious consumers and build long-lasting trust.

Embracing AI responsibly by understanding the risks and challenges is a strategic necessity for sustainable innovation. By aligning AI technologies with organisational goals, organisations can unlock their full potential while mitigating risks and ensuring equitable outcomes.

Developing a governance and risk approach is not only a sensible thing to do to protect the organisation but also enables the organisation to seize opportunities.

Relevant standards and guidance

ISO 42001

ISO/IEC 42001:2023 is an international standard for AI management systems. Like other ISO management system standards, it follows a defined structure that includes many overlaps with other management systems. This means the organisation implementing it can save time and resources on common processes, such as management review, documentation control, etc.

In addition to the clauses that set out requirements for the management system, the Standard includes four annexes for additional detail and guidance:

- Annex A provides the control set, which is intended to act as a reference during the AI risk assessment. It includes what the Standard considers a 'comprehensive' range of controls for AI.
- Annex B provides guidance for implementing the controls in Annex A.
- Annex C outlines potential objectives and risk sources for the AI management system to consider. As AI is still very new for most organisations, this is likely to help frame the AIMS and provide direction during risk management.
- Annex D provides a very brief suggestion as to how the management system might be applied to different industries and sectors. It also describes how the

management system might be integrated with ISO 27001, ISO 27701 and ISO 9001.

The primary advantage of ISO 42001 is that it is one of the first standards for managing AI, and it does so in accordance with well-understood risk management principles. Because ISO standards are widely adopted and accredited certification is accepted around the world, this forms a strong basis for compliance with current and emerging legislation and regulation.

The secondary advantage of ISO 42001 is that it is independently certifiable. An organisation that implements it can have its AIMS audited by an independent certification body, which provides evidence to customers, partners and regulators that the organisation is taking management of AI risk seriously.

ISO 22989

ISO/IEC 22989:2022 provides a standardised set of concepts and terms for discussing AI in ISO standards. This is roughly comparable to ISO 27000 for information security or ISO 9000 for quality management.

Having standardised language helps ensure a common understanding when discussing AI concerns, and can be applied across disciplines, industries and sectors. This is obviously essential for ISO standards.

ISO 22989 is a foundational reference for an AIMS. While ISO 42001 provides some definitions, it's a more limited range of terms and concepts, and benefits from being read in conjunction with ISO 22989.

ISO 23894

ISO/IEC 23894:2023 provides guidance on AI risk management. It isn't specific to ISO 42001, but because it reflects the norms of ISO-based risk management (building on ISO 31000), it can be readily applied to any management system that needs to examine AI risk, such as ISO 27001, ISO 27701 or ISO 42001.

As a supporting standard for AI risk management, it provides guidance on safely developing and using AI. It also offers advice for organisations on integrating risk management into AI activities and business functions.

As a purely guidance standard, it's not mandatory, even when implementing ISO 42001. However, it does offer a wealth of good advice that's worth taking into consideration as part of developing or implementing AI systems and tools.

ISO 38507

ISO/IEC 38507:2022 is interested in the governance of AI within organisations. It's important to note the distinction between management and governance, and how ISO standards treat these structures.

You'll note that, throughout this book, I talk about 'governance' rather than focusing solely on management. This is because it's absolutely essential. Furthermore, ISO management system standards inherently address many elements of governance and provide structures and processes that support governance.

ISO 38507 takes this a little further, providing guidance on how governance functions might address their duties in relation to the use of AI tools and systems. The Standard aims to ensure that AI is used in an effective, efficient and acceptable manner, and that it aligns with the organisation's objectives and stakeholder expectations.

ISO 24030

ISO/IEC TR 24030:2024 sets out example use cases for AI, which is clearly valuable to any organisation considering its options for the technology. It's easy to fall back on ideas like "Well, we can use ChatGPT or Copilot to write our marketing", but AI presents far more opportunities to streamline processes, increase productivity and exploit the data that you already have.

Each use case is based on one submitted by participating experts, and may or may not be based on actual application. The use cases are often quite specific, such as "Real-time segmentation and prediction of plant growth dynamics using low-power embedded systems equipped with AI" for the agricultural sector, or "AI tool for species categorization for wildlife population monitoring" in the public sector.

Each use case is broken down into consistent subsections to ensure each case is properly explained and examined. These subsections include things like objectives, stakeholder and stakeholder considerations, KPIs, threats and vulnerabilities, challenges and issues, etc.

If you're unsure what AI can do for your organisation, this is worth a read.

ISO 24028

ISO/IEC TR 24028:2020 is intended to help organisations identify factors that can affect the trustworthiness of AI systems and tools. It examines vulnerabilities and mitigations, and should prove valuable to developers of AI systems and tools.

The Standard also includes discussions around bias, unpredictability and opaqueness from the perspective of viewing failures in these areas as vulnerabilities. This framing may help organisations understand how to manage such risks during development and implementation of AI systems and tools.

ISO 24028 is most likely to be relevant for organisations looking to develop or adopt AI systems that can be balanced against societal and ethical norms.

ISO 24368

ISO/IEC TR 24368:2022, like ISO 24028, is intended as an examination of one of the problems around AI. In this case, it's an examination of ethical and societal concerns. While there's no shortage of books, papers and studies on ethical and societal concerns around AI, few (if any) approach these from the perspective of an ISO standard and how these concerns might impact a management system.

This leads into the Standard's examination of the more practical aspects of building and using AIs, ethical review frameworks, etc. As an international standard, it also addresses specific concerns related to geographical regions, which may be useful for organisations that operate internationally.

Annex B of the document includes use case studies that illustrate real-world applications of AI and the associated ethical and societal considerations.

ISO 5259 series

ISO/IEC 5259 is a set of standards relating to data quality in AI systems. These standards comprise:

- ISO/IEC 5259-1:2024: An overview of data quality for analytics and machine learning.
- ISO/IEC 5259-2:2024: Data quality measures.
- ISO/IEC 5259-3:2024: Data quality management requirements and guidelines.
- ISO/IEC 5259-4:2024: Data quality process framework.
- ISO/IEC 5259-5:2025: Data quality governance framework.

Altogether, these provide definitions, guidance and a set of requirements for data quality in AI applications. Because the outputs of AI systems can only be as good as the data fed into them, this may be a valuable source of guidance on ensuring the highest-quality data is available for AI systems.

The primary value of the ISO 5259 series will be to establish a solid foundation for data quality management, enhancing the effectiveness and trustworthiness of AI and machine learning systems.

NIST

Artificial Intelligence Risk Management Framework (AI RMF 1.0)

NIST's AI RMF is, like ISO 42001, an attempt to create a framework for managing AI risk. Its approach is to apply four functions at a high level: govern, map, measure and manage.

- Govern refers to the organisation overseeing the whole AI risk management process, which informs and is fed back to by the other functions.
- Map refers to recognising the context and risks related to the use of AI.
- Measure refers to what we might call the 'main' risk management processes of analysing, evaluating or tracking risks.
- Manage refers to the processes around prioritising and acting on risks to reduce their impact or likelihood, as in any other risk management framework.

Each of these functions includes a number of objectives (called 'categories') and practices ('subcategories') that the organisation can put in place as necessary to deal with AI risk. Subcategories are functionally similar in role to controls in ISO 42001.

Like other NIST frameworks, it includes a model for identifying a target state and progress achieving that. This isn't something that ISO offers, but the model is agnostic, so it could be applied to an ISO 42001 project.

Usefully, the RMF also includes appendices that discuss valuable topics, such as how AI risks differ from more traditional software risks.

Unlike ISO 42001, there is no certification programme for the AI RMF. This means that an organisation that wants to prove its credentials for managing AI risk will need to develop some other way of showing that it is taking the risks seriously.

Generative AI Profile (NIST AI 600-1)

NIST's Generative AI Profile is a supplement to the AI RMF, which describes a number of the key risks associated with generative AI. This aims to help organisations dealing with AI risk management as it is still a new area for the discipline.

The document also includes a range of actions that can be applied through the RMF. These are aligned with the categories and subcategories to provide a clear set of actions to address known risks. This a fairly sizeable set of actions, which could provide a lot of useful detail for implementing the RMF.

Secure Software Development Practices for Generative AI and Dual-Use Foundation Models (SP 800-218A)

This document addresses the key risks and vulnerabilities introduced during development and how they can be managed. For organisations not developing their own AI systems, the main value will be to build a stronger understanding of how AI systems are developed. This knowledge can be used to perform better due diligence.

Managing Misuse Risks for Dual-Use Foundation Models (NIST AI 800-1)

This document sets out guidance for developing AI foundation models – AI models trained on large datasets that have a wide range of possible use cases. Because they are relatively unrefined at this stage, it's important for the models to have additional safety measures applied to prevent the models being misused.

Essentially, this is about applying a set of rules for the AI model before users can cause harm, either intentionally or accidentally. The document notes that such misuse could include "using a model to facilitate the development of chemical, biological, radiological, or nuclear weapons; enable offensive cyber-attacks"; and so on.

At the time of writing, this is in its second draft and available for review and public comment. Having said that, it's unlikely to change considerably before it's released (although see below).

It's worth noting that many of these documents were developed in response to an executive order issued by President Biden, and that this executive order has since been repealed by the Trump administration. While the documents remain good sources of guidance, it also wouldn't be surprising if these are withdrawn, replaced or amended to align with whatever new executive orders are issued by President Trump.

FURTHER READING

GRC Solutions is the world's leading publisher for governance and compliance. Our industry-leading pocket guides, books and training resources are written by real-world practitioners and thought leaders. They are used globally by audiences of all levels, from students to C-suite executives.

Our high-quality publications cover all IT governance, risk and compliance frameworks and are available in a range of formats. This ensures our customers can access the information they need in the way they need it.

Other books you may find useful include:

- *Digital Ethics in the Age of AI – Navigating the ethical frontier today and beyond* by Dr Julie Mehan, *https://www.itgovernance.co.uk/shop/product/digital-ethics-in-the-age-of-ai-navigating-the-ethical-frontier-today-and-beyond*
- *IT Governance – An international guide to data security and ISO 27001/ISO 27002,* Eighth edition by Alan Calder and Steve Watkins, *https://www.itgovernance.co.uk/shop/product/it-governance-an-international-guide-to-data-security-and-iso-27001iso-27002-eighth-edition*
- *NIST CSF 2.0 – Your essential introduction to managing cybersecurity risks* by Andrew Pattison, *https://www.itgovernance.co.uk/shop/product/nist-*

*csf-20-your-essential-introduction-to-managing-
cybersecurity-risks*

For more information on GRC Solutions and IT
Governance™, a GRC Solutions Company as well as
branded publishing services, please
visit *https://www.itgovernance.co.uk/*.

Branded publishing

Through our branded publishing service, you can
customise our publications with your organisation's
branding. For more information, please contact:

clientservices-uk@grcsolutions.io

Related services

GRC Solutions offers a comprehensive range of
complementary products and services to help organisations
meet their objectives.

For a full range of resources, please
visit *www.itgovernance.co.uk*.

Training services

GRC Solutions' training programme is built on our
extensive practical experience designing and implementing
management systems based on ISO standards, best practice
and regulations.

Our courses help attendees develop practical skills and
comply with contractual and regulatory requirements. They
also support career development via recognised
qualifications.

Learn more about our training courses and view the full course catalogue at

www.itgovernance.co.uk/training.

Professional services and consultancy

We are a leading global consultancy of IT governance, risk management and compliance solutions. We advise organisations around the world on their most critical issues and present cost-saving and risk-reducing solutions based on international best practice and frameworks.

We offer a wide range of delivery methods to suit all budgets, timescales and preferred project approaches.

Find out how our consultancy services can help your organisation at

www.itgovernance.co.uk/consulting.

Industry news

Want to stay up to date with the latest developments and resources in the IT governance and compliance market? Subscribe to our Security Spotlight newsletter and we will send you mobile-friendly emails with fresh news and features about your preferred areas of interest, as well as unmissable offers and free resources to help you successfully start your project: *www.itgovernance.co.uk/security-spotlight-newsletter.*

EU for product safety is Stephen Evans, The Mill Enterprise Hub, Stagreenan, Drogheda, Co. Louth, A92 CD3D, Ireland. (servicecentre@itgovernance.eu)